# HOW CAN I EXPERIMENT WITH ... ?

# A WEDGE

## David and Patricia Armentrout

Rourke
Publishing LLC
Vero Beach, Florida 32964

www.rourkepublishing.com


PHOTO CREDITS: ©Armentrout pgs 4, 9, 29; ©David French Photography pgs 14, 17, 20, 23, 25, 27; ©Image 100 Ltd. Cover; ©Digital Vision Ltd. pgs 11, 18; ©Painet, Inc.7, 13.

Cover: *Teeth work like tiny wedges.*

Editor: Frank Sloan

Cover design: Nicola Stratford

Series Consulting Editor: Henry Rasof, a former editor with Franklin Watts, has edited many science books for children and young adults.

**Library of Congress Cataloging-in-Publication Data**


Armentrout, David, 1962-
  How can I experiment with simple machines? A wedge / David and Patricia Armentrout.
       p. cm.
Summary: Defines wedges, explains their functions, and suggests simple experiments to demonstrate how they work.
Includes bibliographical references and index.
  ISBN 1-58952-337-7
  1. Wedges—Juvenile literature. [1. Wedges—Experiments. 2. Experiments.]  I. Title: Wedge. II. Armentrout, Patricia, 1960- III. Title.
   TJ1201.W44 A758 2002
   621.8—dc21

                                                              2002007653

**Printed in the USA**

W/W

# Table of Contents

**Wedge** (WEJ) — a simple machine that acts like a moving inclined plane

*An iron wedge can be used to split logs.*

# Working Machines

The world we live in is much different than the world our early ancestors lived in. We have many machines that make our work easier.

Much of the work our ancestors did was for basic survival. Hunting and growing food, building shelters, and staying warm were daily challenges. Thanks to modern machines, we no longer have to spend all of our energy on survival. Machines make our work easier and they save us time. Most modern machines have one thing in common—they are made up of simple machines.

*Machines save time.*

# Simple Machines

The wedge, the wheel, the screw, the **inclined plane**, the pulley, and the lever are simple machines. They are simple because they have few parts.

Do you think prehistoric people used simple machines? Yes, they did. Early hunters discovered that a sharp wedge shape on the end of a pole made a dangerous weapon. The sharp wedge was also used to scrape animal skins, dig holes, and split logs. Can you think of any other simple machines that prehistoric people may have used?

*Early stone tools prove that prehistoric people used simple machines.*

# The Wedge

An inclined plane is a flat sloped surface. A wedge is like an inclined plane with one or two sloped sides. A wedge is shaped like a triangle with a wide end and a narrow end. A wedge acts as a moving inclined plane. Applying force on the wide end of the wedge will drive the narrow end into an object or between two objects.

Machines make use of the wedge to cut, to split, and to tighten, or hold. Machines that use wedges give us a **mechanical advantage**. This means they can help us do work with less effort.

*A knife is a wedge that can cut or split.*

# Wedges That Split

A wedge can be used to split something apart. The shape of a wedge makes it the perfect tool for the job.

Imagine you have a stack of big round logs. The logs are too big to fit in your fireplace. Your job is to split the logs into usable pieces. You need a wedge and a sledgehammer. First you place the sharp narrow end of the wedge on the top flat surface of a log. Next, you strike the wide end of the wedge with your hammer. With each strike of the hammer, the wedge is driven further into the log, splitting it apart.

Your teeth are wedges, too. They are used to cut or split your food into small, manageable pieces.

*Front teeth are sharp and shaped like a wedge.*

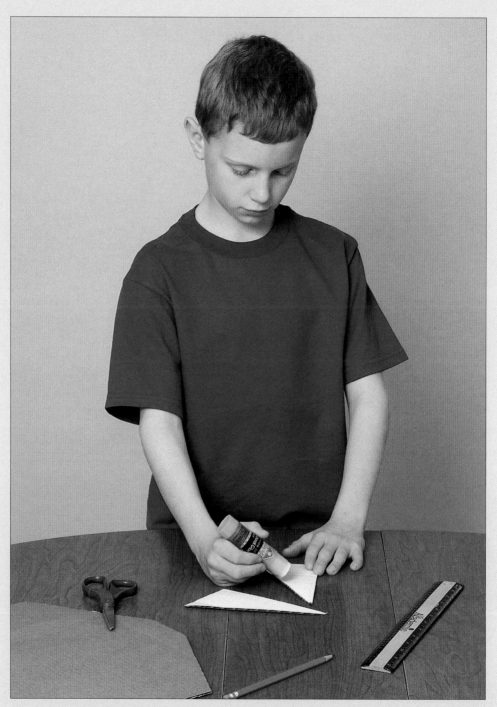

**14**     *A wedge is easy to make.*

# Make a Wedge

**You will need:**

- ruler
- pencil
- sheet of thick cardboard
- scissors
- glue stick

Using the ruler and the pencil, measure and draw a right triangle at one corner of the cardboard. Make the base 6 inches (15 centimeters) and the height 3 inches (7.6 cm). Measure and draw a second triangle the same size from another corner of the cardboard. Use the scissors to carefully cut out the triangles.

Using the glue stick, glue one triangle to the other, forming one thick right triangle. The triangle is a wedge. Use the wedge for the next experiment.

# Experiment with a Wedge

**You will need:**

- 2 books
- table
- friend
- wedge

Stack the books on the table. Have your friend hold the back sides of the books so they do not slide. Place the narrow end of the wedge between the books. Gently push the wedge in partway. Notice how the wedge splits the books apart.

Push the wedge in further. As the wedge is pushed further, the book on top is lifted higher. The amount of force needed to push the wedge in is less than the force you would need to lift the books without a wedge.

*A wedge works like a moving inclined plane.*

# Wedges That Cut

You don't have to look far to find a cutting wedge. The blade on a kitchen knife is a great example. The thin blade slices easily through food.

A carpenter's saw is a cutting wedge, too. Each tooth on the saw blade is a wedge. As the carpenter draws the saw back and forth over the wood, the teeth cut the fibers that hold the wood together.

Some cutting tools are wedges and levers combined. Scissors and nail clippers are double levers that have two sharp cutting blades.

*Scissors are a combination of two simple machines.*

*It's hard to cut out shapes without using a wedge.*

20    *It doesn't take much effort to cut through modeling clay with a wedge.*

# Experiment with a Cutting Wedge

**You will need:**

- modeling clay
- plastic knife

Flatten some of the modeling clay so that it is about 1/2 inch (1-2 cm) thick. Using your fingers, try to cut a triangle shape, a circle shape, and a square shape out of the modeling clay. It's not easy because fingers are round and blunt. Try making the shapes again using the plastic knife. Was it easier to cut the shapes using the plastic knife? The blade of the knife is a wedge that makes cutting easier.

# Wedges That Hold or Tighten

Wedges not only split things apart, they can also be used to hold or tighten. A doorstop is a wedge that can hold a door in place. When you slide the doorstop under a door, the wedge is forced between the bottom of the door and the floor. More force on the doorstop causes it to wedge in and hold even tighter.

The sharp tip on a nail is a wedge. With the help of a hammer, the nail can be driven into wood very easily. A nail that passes from one piece of wood into another will hold them both tightly together.

*The wedge makes a perfect doorstop.*

# Shape Matters!

Try this experiment:

**You will need:**

- adult helper
- safety glasses
- bolt
- piece of wood
- hammer

Have the adult supervise while you do this experiment.

Put on the safety glasses. Place the bolt on the piece of wood and hold it steady. Being careful not to hit your fingers, use the hammer to try to drive the bolt into the wood.

Was it hard to hammer the bolt into the wood? Look at the shape on the tip of the bolt. It is round and flat. Can you think of a shape that would make the job easier?

*It would take a great deal of effort to hammer a flat-tipped bolt into wood.*

# Using a Wedge to Hold

**You will need:**

- adult helper
- safety glasses
- nail
- piece of wood
- hammer

Have the adult supervise while you do this experiment.

Put on the safety glasses. Place the nail on the piece of wood and hold it steady. Being careful not to hit your fingers, use the hammer to try to drive the nail into the wood.

Did the nail enter the wood easier than the bolt? The nail has a sharp, pointed tip. The tip of the nail is a wedge that can easily be driven into a piece of wood. Once the nail has been driven, it holds tight.

*A nail makes a much better wedge than a bolt.*

# Complex Machines

A knife, a shovel, an ax, and a nail are wedges that make work easier. They all use a sloped surface to give us a mechanical advantage. They all act as moving inclined planes.

You can find wedges in more **complex** machines. A sewing machine has a wedge called a needle. A bulldozer has a wedge called a shovel. A chain saw has a wedge called a chain.

Can you think of any other machines that use the wedge?

*Complex machines, like chain saws, have many parts.*

# Glossary

**complex** (KAHM pleks) — made up of many parts

**inclined plane** (IN klynd PLAYN) — a flat sloping surface used to make work easier

**mechanical advantage** (mi KAN eh kul ad VAN tij) — what you gain when a simple machine allows you to use less effort